The Ascension of Isaiah

By Isaiah

Copyright © 2022 Lamp of Trismegistus. All rights reserved. No part of this publication may be reproduced or transmitted in any form or by any means, electronic or mechanical, including photocopying, recording, or by any information storage and retrieval system, without permission in writing from Lamp of Trismegistus. Reviewers may quote brief passages.

ISBN: 978-1-63118-620-2

Christian Apocrypha Series

Other Books in this Series and Related Titles

The Book of Wisdom of Solomon by King Solomon (978-1-63118-502-1)

The Apocalypse of Peter by Peter (978-1-63118-527-4)

The Gospel of the Nativity of Mary by St. Matthew (978-1-63118-448-2)

The Vision of Saint Paul the Apostle by Paul (978-1-63118-526-7)

Early Translation of the Acts of the Apostles by Luke (978-1-63118-521-2)

The Hymn of Jesus by G. R. S. Mead (978-1-63118-409-3)

Psalms of Solomon by King Solomon (978-1-63118-439-0)

The First and Second Gospels of the Infancy of Jesus Christ (978-1-63118-415-4)

The Book of Parables by Enoch (978-1-63118-429-1)

The Testament of Abraham by Abraham (978-1-63118-441-3)

The Lives of Adam and Eve by Moses (978-1-63118-414-7)

Fourth Book of Maccabees by Josephus (978-1-63118-562-5)

Book of the Watchers by Enoch (978-1-63118-615-8)

Lost Chapters of the Book of Daniel and Related Writings (978-1-63118-417-8)

The Testament of Moses by Moses (978-1-63118-440-6)

Testaments of the Twelve Patriarchs (978-1-63118-579-3)

The Story of Ahikar by Ahiqar (978-1-63118-561-8)

The Odes of Solomon by King Solomon (978-1-63118-503-8)

Book of Dreams by Enoch (978-1-63118-437-6)

Kali the Mother by Sister Nivedita (978-1-63118-558-8)

The Book of Astronomical Secrets by Enoch (978-1-63118-443-7)

Audio Versions are also Available on Audible, Amazon and Apple

Other Books in this Series and Related Titles

The Hidden Mysteries of Christianity by Annie Besant (978–1–63118–534–2)

Second Book of Enoch by Enoch (978-1-63118-617-2)

The Hymns of Hermes by G. R. S. Mead (978-1-63118-405-5)

Freemasonry and the Egyptian Mysteries by C. W. Leadbeater (978-1-63118-456-7)

The Sepher Yetzirah and the Qabalah by M P Hall (978-1-63118-481-9)

Love and Death by Sri Aurobindo (978-1-63118-557-1)

The Historic, Mythic and Mystic Christ by Annie Besant (978–1–63118–533–5)

The Fourth-Gospel and Synoptical Problem by G R S Mead (978–1–63118–576–2)

Masonic Symbolism of King Solomon's Temple by A Mackey &c (978-1-63118-442-0)

The Crest-Jewel of Wisdom by Adi Shankara (978-1-63118-475-8)

The Old Past Master by Carl H Claudy (978-1-63118-464-2)

The Brotherhood of Religions by Annie Besant (978–1–63118–563–2)

What Theosophy Does for Us by C W Leadbeater (978–1–63118–574–8)

Buddhist Psalms by Shinran (978-1-63118-465-9)

Catholicism, Yoga and Hinduism by Hartmann &c (978-1-63118-478-9)

Masonic Symbolism of Easter and the Christ in Masonry (978-1-63118-434-5)

Tao Te Ching & Commentary by Lao Tzu & C Johnston (978-1-63118-495-6)

Ancient Mysteries and Secret Societies by M P Hall (978-1-63118-410-9)

The Golden Verses of Pythagoras: Five Translations (978-1-63118-479-6)

Freemasonry & Catholicism by Max Heindel (978-1-63118-508-3)

A Few Masonic Sermons by A. C. Ward &c (978-1-63118-435-2)

Audio versions are also available on Audible, Amazon and Apple

Table of Contents

Introduction...7

Chapter 1...9

Chapter 2...11

Chapter 3...14

Chapter 4...18

Chapter 5...21

Chapter 6...23

Chapter 7...25

Chapter 8...30

Chapter 9...33

Chapter 10...38

Chapter 11...42

SERIES INTRODUCTION

The Apocrypha are a loosely knit series of books, written by early vanguards of Christianity (covering the eras of both the old and new testaments), and which comprise somewhere between about a dozen to several hundred titles, depending on whom you ask and how that person defines "Apocrypha." A small selection of these can still be found included in the Catholic bible, while a majority of the books in question, were abandoned by church officials in the early centuries of Christianity. Many of these apocryphal books were originally considered canon by early followers of Christ, in the first four centuries following his birth. It wasn't until the meeting of the Council of Nicaea in 325, that Emperor Constantine and a group of roughly 300 church bishops, gathered together with the goal of defining, standardizing and unifying an otherwise splintering Christianity, that many of these writings ceased to be included in the newly established canon. Enjoy then, this book as an example, of just one of the many books of the Christian Apocrypha, and be sure to check out other titles in this series.

The Ascension of Isaiah

CHAPTER 1

AND it came to pass in the twenty-sixth year of the reign of Hezediah king of Judah that he called Manasseh his son. Now he was his only one.

2. And he called him into the presence of Isaiah the son of Amoz the prophet, and into the presence of Josab the son of Isaiah, in order to deliver unto him the words of righteousness which the king himself had seen:

3. And of the eternal judgments and torments of Gehenna, and of the prince of this world, and of his angels, and his authorities and his powers.

4. And the words of the faith of the Beloved which he himself had seen in the fifteenth year of his reign during his illness.

5. And he delivered unto him the written words which Samnas the scribe had written, and also those which Isaiah, the son of Amoz, had given to him, and also to the prophets, that they might write and store up with him what he himself had seen in the king's house regarding the judgment of the angels, and the destruction of this world, and regarding the garments of the saints and their going forth, and regarding their transformation and the persecution and ascension of the Beloved.

6. In the twentieth year of the reign of Hezekiah, Isaiah had seen the words of this prophecy and had delivered them to Josab his son. And whilst he (Hezekiah) gave commands, Josab the son of Isaiah standing by.

7. Isaiah said to Hezekiah the king, but not in the presence of Manasseh only did he say unto him: `As the Lord liveth, and th3e Spirit which speaketh in me liveth, all these commands and these words will be made of none effect by Manasseh thy son, and through the agency of his hands I shall depart mid the torture of my body.

8. And Sammael Malchira will serve Manasseh, and execute all his desire, and he will become a follower of Beliar rather than of me:

9. And many in Jerusalem and in Judea he will cause to abandon the true faith, and Beliar will dwell in Manasseh, and by his hands I shall be sawn asunder.'

10. And when Hezekiah heard these words he wept very bitterly, and rent his garments, and placed earth upon his head, and fell on his face.

11. And Isaiah said unto him: `The counsel of Sammael against Manasseh is consummated: nought will avail thee."

12. And on that day Hezekiah resolved in his heart to slay Manasseh his son.

13. And Isaiah said to Hezekiah: `The Beloved hath made of none effect thy design, and the purpose of thy heart will not be accomplished, for with this calling have I been called and I shall inherit the heritage of the Beloved.'

CHAPTER 2

AND it came to pass after that Hezekiah died and Manasseh became king, that he did not remember the commands of Hezekiah his father, but forgat them, and Sammael abode in Manasseh and clung fast to him.

2. And Manasseh forsook the service of the God of his father, and he served Satan and his angels and his powers.

3. And he turned aside the house of his father, which had been before the face of Hezekiah (from) the words of wisdom and from the service of God.

4. And Manasseh turned aside his heart to serve Beliar; for the angel of lawlessness, who is the ruler of this world, is Beliar, whose name is Mantanbuchus. and he delighted in Jerusalem because of Manasseh, and he made him strong in apostatizing (Israel) and in the lawlessness which were spread abroad in Jerusalem.

5. And witchcraft and magic increased and divination and auguration, and fornication, a [and adultery], and the persecution of the righteous by Manasseh and [Belachira, and] Tobia the Canaanite, and John of Anatoth, an by (Zadok) the chief of the works.

6. And the rest of the acts, behold they are written in the book of the Kings of Judah and Israel.

7. And, when Isaiah, the son of Amoz, saw the lawlessness which was being perpetrated in Jerusalem and the worship of Satan and his wantonness, he withdrew from Jerusalem and settled in Bethlehem of Judah.

8. And there also there was much lawlessness, and withdrawing from Bethlehem he settled on a mountain in a desert place.

9. And Micaiah the prophet, and the aged Ananias, and Joel and Habakkuk, and his son Josab, and many of the faithful who believed in the ascension into heaven, withdrew and settled on the mountain.

10. They were all clothed with garments of hair, and they were all prophets. And they had nothing with them but were naked, and they all lamented with a great lamentation because of the going astray of Israel.

11. And these eat nothing save wild herbs which they gathered on the mountains, and having cooked them, they lived thereon together with Isaiah the prophet. And they spent two years of days on the mountains and hills.

12. And after this, whilst they were in the desert, there was a certain man in Samaria named Belchira, of the family of Zedekiah, the son of Chenaan, a false prophet, whose dwelling was in Bethlehem. Now Hezekiah the son of Chanani, who was the brother of his father, and in the days of Ahab, king of Israel, had been the teacher of the 400. prophets of Baal, had himself smitten and reproved Micaiah the son of Amada the prophet.

13. And he, Micaiah, had been reproved by Ahab and cast into prison. (And he was) with Zedekiah the prophet: they were with Ahaziah the son of Ahab, king in Samaria.

14. And Elijah the prophet of Tebon of Gilead was reproving Ahaziah and Samaria, and prophesied regarding Ahaziah that he should die on his bed of sickness, and that Samaria should be delivered into the had of Leba Nasr because he had slain the prophets of God.

15. And when the false prophets, who were with Ahaziah the son of Ahab and their teacher Jalerjas of Mount Joel, had heard-

16. Now he was a brother of Zedekiah - when they persuaded Ahaziah the king of Aguaron and (slew) Micaiah.

CHAPTER 3

AND Belchira recognized and saw the place of Isaiah and the prophets who were with him; for he dwelt in the region of Bethlehem, and was an adherent of Manasseh. And he prophesied falsely in Jerusalem, and many belonging to Jerusalem were confederate with him, and he was a Samaritan.

2. And it came to pass when Alagar Zagar, king of Assyria, had come and captive, and led them away to the mountains of the medes and the rivers of Tazon;

3. This (Belchira), whilst still a youth, had escaped and come to Jerusalem in the days of Hezekiah king of Judah, but he walked not in the ways of his father of Samaria; for he feared Hezekiah.

4. And he was found in the days of Hezekiah speaking words of lawlessness in Jerusalem.

5. And the servants of Hezekiah accused him, and he made his escape to the region of Bethlehem. And they persuaded...

6. And Belchira accused Isaiah and the prophets who were with him, saying: `Isaiah and those who are with him prophesy against Jerusalem and against the cities of Judah that they shall be laid waste and (against the children of Judah and) Benjamin also that they shall go into captivity, and also against thee, O lord the king, that thou shalt go (bound) with hooks and iron chains':

7. But they prophesy falsely against Israel and Judah.

8. And Isaiah himself hath said: `I see more than Moses the prophet.'

9. But Moses said: `No man can see God and live'; and Isaiah hath said: `I have seen God and behold I live.'

10. Know, therefore, O king, that he is lying. And Jerusalem also he hath called Sodom, and the princes of Judah and Jerusalem he hath declared to be the people of Gomorrah. And he brought many accusations against Isaiah and the prophets before Manasseh.

11. But Beliar dwelt in the heart of Manasseh and in the heart of the princes of Judah and Benjamin and of the eunuchs and of the councillors of the king.

12. And the words of Belchira pleased him [exceedingly], and he sent and seized Isaiah.

13. For Beliar was in great wrath against Isaiah by reason of the vision, and because of the exposure wherewith he had exposed Sammael, and because through him the going forth of the Beloved from the seventh heaven had been made known, and His transformation and His descent and the likeness into which He should be transformed (that is) the likeness of man, and the persecution wherewith he should be persecuted, and the torturers wherewith the children of Israel should torture Him, and the coming of His twelve disciples, and the teaching, and that He should before the sabbath be crucified upon the tree, and should be crucified together with wicked men, and that He should be buried in the sepulchre,

14. And the twelve who were with Him should be offended because of Him: and the watch of those who watched the sepulchre:

15. And the descent of the angel of the Christian Church, which is in the heavens, whom He will summon in the last days.

16. And that (Gabriel) the angel of the Holy Spirit, and Michael, the chief of the holy angels, on the third day will open the sepulchre:

17. And the Beloved sitting on their shoulders will come forth and send out His twelve disciples;

18. And they will teach all the nations and every tongue of the resurrection of the Beloved, and those who believe in His cross will be saved, and in His ascension into the seventh heaven whence He came:

19. And that many who believe in Him will speak through the Holy Spirit:

20. And many signs and wonders will be wrought in those days.

21. And afterwards, on the eve of His approach, His disciples will forsake the teachings of the Twelve Apostles, and their faith, and their love and their purity.

22. And there will be much contention on the eve of [His advent and] His approach.

23. And in those days many will love office, though devoid of wisdom.

24. And there will be many lawless elders, and shepherds dealing wrongly by their own sheep, and they will ravage (them) owing to their not having holy shepherds.

25. And many will change the honour of the garments of the saints for the garments of the covetous, and there will be much respect of persons in those days and lovers of the honour of this world.

26. And there will be much slander and vainglory at the approach of the Lord, and the Holy Spirit will withdraw from many.

27. And there will not be in those days many prophets, nor those who speak trustworthy words, save one here and there in divers places,

28. On account of the spirit of error and fornication and of vainglory, and of covetousness, which shall be in those, who will be called servants of that One and in those who will receive that One.

29. And there will be great hatred in the shepherds and elders towards each other.

30. For there will be great jealousy in the last days; for every one will say what is pleasing in his own eyes.

31. And they will make of none effect the prophecy of the prophets which were before me, and these my visions also will they make of none effect, in order to speak after the impulse of their own hearts.

CHAPTER 4

AND now Hezekiah and Josab my son, these are the days of the completion of the world.

2. After it is consummated, Beliar the great ruler, the king of this world, will descend, who hath ruled it since it came into being; yea, he will descent from his firmament in the likeness of a man, a lawless king, the slayer of his mother: who himself (even) this king.

3. Will persecute the plant which the Twelve Apostles of the Beloved have planted. Of the Twelve one will be delivered into his hands.

4. This ruler in the form of that king will come and there will come and there will come with him all the powers of this world, and they will hearken unto him in all that he desires.

5. And at his word the sun will rise at night and he will make the moon to appear at the sixth hour.

6. And all that he hath desired he will do in the world: he will do and speak like the Beloved and he will say: "I am God and before me there has been none."

7. And all the people in the world will believe in him.

8. And they will sacrifice to him and they will serve him saying: "This is God and beside him there is no other."

9. And they greater number of those who shall have been associated together in order to receive the Beloved, he will turn aside after him.

10. And there will be the power of his miracles in every city and region.

11. And he will set up his image before him in every city.

12. And he shall bear sway three years and seven months and twenty-seven days.

13. And many believers and saints having seen Him for whom they were hoping, who was crucified, Jesus the Lord Christ, [after that I, Isaiah, had seen Him who was crucified and ascended] and those also who were believers in Him - of these few in those days will be left as His servants, while they flee from desert to desert, awaiting the coming of the Beloved.

14. And after (one thousand) three hundred and thirty-two days the Lord will come with His angels and with the armies of the holy ones from the seventh heaven with the glory of the seventh heaven, and He will drag Beliar into Gehenna and also his armies.

15. And He will give rest of the godly whom He shall find in the body in this world, [and the sun wil be ashamed]:

16. And to all who because of (their) faith in Him have execrated Beliar and his kings. But the saints will come with the Lord with their garments which are (now) stored up on high in the seventh heaven: with the Lord they will come, whose spirits are clothed, they will descend and be present in the world, and He will strengthen those, who have been found in the body, together with the saints, in the garments of the saints, and the Lord will minister to those who have kept watch in this world.

17. And afterwards they will turn themselves upward in their garments, and their body will be left in the world.

18. Then the voice of the Beloved will in wrath rebuke the things of heaven and the things of earth and the things of earth and the mountains and the hills and the cities and the desert and the

forests and the angel of the sun and that of the moon, and all things wherein Beliar manifested himself and acted openly in this world, and there will be [a resurrection and] a judgment in their midst in those days, and the Beloved will cause fire to go forth from Him, and it will consume all the godless, and they will be as though they had not been created.

19. And the rest of the words of the vision is written in the vision of Babylon.

20. And the rest of the vision regarding the Lord, behold, it is written in three parables according to my words which are written in the book which I publicly prophesied.

21. And the descent of the Beloved into Sheol, behold, it is written in the section, where the Lord says: "Behold my Son will understand." And all these things, behold they are written [in the Psalms] in the parables of David, the son of Jesse, and in the Proverbs of Solomon his son, and in the words of Korah, and Ethan the Israelite, and in the words of Asaph, and in the rest of the Psalms also which the angel of the Spirit inspired.

22. (Namely) in those which have not the name written, and in the words of my father Amos, and of Hosea the prophet, and of Micah and Joel and Nahum and Jonah and Obadiah and Habakkuk and Haggai and Malachi, and in the words of Joseph the Just and in the words of Daniel.

CHAPTER 5

ON account of these visions, therefore, Beliar was wroth with Isaiah, and he dwelt in the heart of Manasseh and he sawed him in sunder with a wooden saw.

2. And when Isaiah was being sawn in sunder, Belchira stood up, accusing him, and all the false prophets stood up, laughing and rejoicing because of Isaiah.

3. And Belchira, with the aid of Mechembechus, stood up before Isaiah, [laughing] deriding;

4. And Belchira said to Isaiah: 'Say, "I have lied in all that I have spoken, and likewise the ways of Manasseh are good and right.

5. And the ways also of Belchira and of his associates are good."

6. And this he said to him when he began to be sawn in sunder.

7. But Isaiah was (absorbed) in a vision of the Lord, and though his eyes were open, he saw them (not).

8. And Belchira spake thus to Isaiah: "Say what I say unto thee and I will turn their hearts, and I will compel Manasseh and the princes of Judah and the people and all Jerusalem to reverence thee.

9. And Isaiah answered and said: "So far as I have utterance (I say): Damned and accused be thou and all they powers and all thy house.

10. For thou canst not take (from me) aught save the skin of my body."

11. And they seized and sawed in sunder Isaiah, the son of Amoz, with a wooden saw.

12. And Manasseh and Belchira and the false prophets and the princes and the people [and] all stood looking on.

13. And to the prophets who were with him he said before he had been sawn in sunder: "Go ye to the region of Tyre and Sidon; for for me only hath God mingled the cup."

14. And when Isaiah was being sawn in sunder, he neither cried aloud nor wept, but his lips spake with the Holy Spirit until he was sawn in twain.

15. This, Beliar did to Isaiah through Belchira and Manasseh; for Sammael was very wrathful against Isaiah from the days of Hezekiah, king of Judah, on account of the things which he had seen regarding the Beloved.

16. And on account of the destruction of Sammael, which he had seen through the Lord, while Hezekiah his father was still king. And he did according to the will of Satan.

CHAPTER 6

The Vision Which Isaiah the Son of Amoz Saw:

In the twentieth year of the reign of Hezekiah, king of Judah, came Isaiah the son of Amoz, and Josab the son of Isaiah to Hezekiah to Jerusalem from Galgala.

2. And (having entered) he sat down on the couch of the king, and they brought him a seat, but he would not sit (thereon).

3. And when Isaiah began to speak the words of faith and truth with King Hezekiah, all the princes of Israel were seated and the eunuchs and the councillors of the king. And there were there forty prophets and sons of the prophets: they had come from the villages and from the mountains and the plains when they had heard that Isaiah was coming from Galgala to Hezekiah.

4. And they had come to salute him and to hear his words.

5. And that he might place his hands upon them, and that they might prophesy and that he might hear their prophecy: and they were all before Isaiah.

6. And when Isaiah was speaking to Hezekiah the words of truth and faith, they all heard a door which one had opened and the voice of the Holy Spirit.

7. And the king summoned all the prophets and all the people who were found there, and they came. and Macaiah and the aged Ananias and Joel and Josab sat on his right hand (and on the left).

8. And it came to pass when they had all heard the voice of the Holy Spirit, they all worshipped on their knees, and glorified the God of truth, the Most High who is in the upper world and who sits on High the Holy One and who rest among His holy ones.

9. And they gave glory to Him who had thus bestowed a door in an alien world had bestowed (it) on a man.

10. And as he was speaking in the Holy Spirit in the hearing of all, he became silent and his mind was taken up from him and he saw not the men that stood before him.

11. Though his eyes indeed were open. Moreover his lips were silent and the mind in his body was taken up from him.

12. But his breath was in him; for he was seeing a vision.

13. And the angel who was sent to make him see was not of this firmament, nor was he of the angels of glory of this world, but he had come from the seventh heaven.

14. And the people who stood near did (not) think, but the circle of the prophets (did), that the holy Isaiah had been taken up.

15. And the vision which the holy Isaiah saw was not from this world but from the world which is hidden from the flesh.

16. And after Isaiah had seen this vision, he narrated it to Hezekiah, and to Josab his son and to the other prophets who had come.

17. But the leaders and the eunuchs and the people did not hear, but only Samna the scribe, and Ijoaqem, and Asaph the recorder; for these also were doers of righteousness, and the sweet smell of the Spirit was upon them. But the people had not heard; for Micaiah and Josab his son had caused them to go forth, when the wisdom of this world had been taken form him and he became as one dead.

CHAPTER 7

AND the vision which Isaiah saw, he told to Hezekiah and Josab his son and Micaiah and the rest of the prophets, (and) said:

2. At this moment, when I prophesied according to the (words) heard which ye heard, I saw a glorious angel not like unto the glory of the angels which I used always to see, but possessing such glory ad position that I cannot describe the glory of that angel.

3. And having seized me by my hand he raised me on high, and I said unto him: "Who art thou, and what is thy name, and whither art thou raising me on high? for strength was given me to speak with him."

4. And he said unto me: "When I have raised thee on high [though the (various) degrees] and made thee see the vision, on account of which I have been sent, then thou wilt understand who I am: but my name thou dost not know.

5. Because thou wilt return into this thy body, but whither I am raising thee on high, thou wilt see; for for this purpose have I been sent."

6. And I rejoiced because he spake courteously to me.

7. And he said unto me: "Hast thou rejoiced because I have spoken courteously to thee?" And he said: "And thou wilt see how a grater also that I am will speak courteously and peaceably with thee."

8. And His Father also who is greater thou wilt see; for for this purpose have I been sent from the seventh heaven in order to explain all these things unto thee."

9. And we ascended to the firmament, I and he, and there I saw Sammael and his hosts, and there was great fighting therein and the angels of Satan were envying one another.

10. And as above so on the earth also; for the likeness of that which is in the firmament is here ont he earth.

11. And I said unto the angel (who was with me): "(What is this war and) what is this envying?"

12. And he said unto me: "So has it been since this world was made until now, and this war (will continue) till He, whom thou shalt see will come and destroy him."

13. And afterwards he caused me to ascend (to that which is) above the firmament: which is the (first) heaven.

14. And there I saw a throne in the midst, and on his right and on his left were angels.

15. And (the angels on the left were) not like unto the angels who stood on the right, but those who stood on the right had the greater glory, and they all praised with one voice, and there was a throne in the midst, and those who were out he left gave praise after them; but their voice was not such as the voice of those on the right, nor their praise like the praise of those.

16. And I asked the angel who conducted me, and I said unto him: "To whom is this praise sent?"

17. And he said unto me: "(it is sent) to the praise of (Him who sitteth in) the seventh heaven: to Him who rests in the holy world, and to His Beloved, whence I have been sent to thee. [Thither is it sent.]"

18. And again, he made me to ascend to the second heaven. now the height of that heaven is the same as from the haven to the earth [and to the firmament].

19. And (I saw there, as) in the first heaven, angels on the right and on the left, and a throne in the midst, and the praise of the angels in the second heaven; and he who sat on the throne in the second heaven was more glorious than all (the rest).

20. And there was great glory in the second heaven, and the praise also was not like the praise of those who were in the first heaven.

21. And I fell on my face to worship him, but he angel who conducted me did not permit me, but said unto me: "Worship neither throne nor angel which belongs to the six heavens - for for this cause I was sent to conduct thee j- until I tell thee in the seventh heaven.

22. For above all the heavens and their angels has thy throne been placed, and thy garments and thy crown which thou shalt see."

23. And I rejoiced with great joy, that those who love the Most High and His Beloved will afterwards ascend thither by the angel of the Holy Spirit.

24. And he raise me to the third heaven, and in like manner I saw those upon the right and upon the left, and there was a throne there in the midst; but the memorial of this world is there unheard of.

25. And I said to the angel who was with me; for the glory of my appearance was undergoing transformation as I ascended to each heaven in turn: "Nothing of the vanity of that world is here named."

26. And he answered me, and said unto me: "Nothing is named on account of its weakness, and nothing is hidden there of what is done."

27. And I wished to learn how it is know, and he answered me saying: "When I have raised thee to the seventh heaven whence I was sent, to that which is above these, then thou shalt know that there is nothing hidden from the thrones and from those who dwell in the heavens and from the angels. And the praise wherewith they praised and glory of him who sat on the throne was great, and the glory of the angels on the right hand and on the left was beyond that of the heaven which was below them.

28. And again he raised me to the fourth heaven, and the height from the third to the height from the third to the forth heaven was greater than from the earth to the firmament.

29. And there again I saw those who were on the right hand and those who were on the left, and him who sat on the throne was in the midst, and there also they were praising.

30. And the praise and glory of the angels on the right was greater than that of those on the left.

31. And again the glory of him who sat on the throne was greater than that of the angels on the right, and their glory was beyond that of those who were below.

32. And he raised me to the fifth heaven.

33. And again I saw those upon the right hand and on the left, and him who sat on the throne possessing greater glory that those of the forth heaven.

34. And the glory of those on the right hand was greater than that of those on the left [from the third to the fourth].

35. And the glory of him who was on the throne was greater than that of the angels on the right hand.

36. And their praise was more glorious than that of the fourth heaven.

37. And I praised Him, who is not named and the Only-begotten who dwelleth in the heavens, whose name is not known to any flesh, who has bestowed such glory on the several heaves, and who makes great the glory of the angels, and more excellent the glory of Him who sitteth on the throne.

CHAPTER 8

AND again he raised me into the air of the sixth heaven, and I saw such glory as I had not seen in the five heavens.

2. For I saw angels possessing great glory.

3. And the praise there was holy and wonderful.

4. And I said to the angel who conducted me: "What is this which I see, my Lord?"

5. And he said: "I am not thy lord, but thy fellow servant."

6. And again I asked him, and I said unto him: "Why are there not angelic fellow servants (on the left)?"

7. And he said: "From the sixth heaven there are no longer angels on the left, nor a throne set in the midst, but (they are directed) by the power of the seventh heaven, where dwelleth He that is not named and the Elect One, whose name has not been made known, and none of the heavens can learn His name.

8. For it is He alone to whose voice all the heavens and thrones give answer. I have therefore been empowered and sent to raise thee here that thou mayest see this glory.

9. And that thou mayest see the Lord of all those heavens and these thrones.

10. Undergoing (successive) transformation until He resembles your form and likeness.

11. I indeed say unto thee, Isaiah; No man about to return into a body of that world has ascended or seen what thou seest or perceived what thou hast perceived and what thou wilt see.

12. For it has been permitted to thee in the lot of the Lord to come hither. [And from thence comes the power of the sixth heaven and of the air]."

13. And I magnified my Lord with praise, in that through His lot I should come hither.

14. And he said: "Hear, furthermore, therefore, this also from thy fellow servant: when from the body by the will of God thou hast ascended hither, then thou wilt receive the garment which thou seest, and likewise other numbered garments laid up (there) thou wilt see.

15. And then thou wilt become equal to the angels of the seventh heaven.

16. And he raised me up into the sixth heaven, and there were no (angels) on the left, nor a throne in the midst, but all had one appearance and their (power of) praise was equal.

17. And (power) was given to me also, and I also praised along with them and that angel also, and our praise was like theirs.

18. And there they all named the primal Father and His Beloved, the Christ, and the Holy Spirit, all with one voice.

19. And (their voice) was not like the voice of the angels in the five heavens.

20. [Nor like their discourse] but the voice was different there, and there was much light there.

21. And then, when I was in the sixth heaven I thought the light which I had seen in the five heavens to be but darkness.

22. And I rejoiced and praised Him who hath bestowed such lights on those who wait for His promise.

23. And I besought the angel who conducted me that I should not henceforth return to the carnal world.

24. I say indeed unto you, Hezekiah and Josab my son and Micaiah, that there is much darkness here.

25. And the angel who conducted me discovered what I thought and said: "If in this light thou dost rejoice, how much more wilt thou rejoice, when in the seventh heaven thou seest the light where is the Lord and His Beloved [whence I have been sent, who is to be called "Son" in this world.

26. Not (yet) hath been manifested he shall be in the corruptible world] and the garments, and the thrones, and the crowns which are laid up for the righteous, for those who trust in that Lord who will descend in your form. For the light which is there is great and wonderful.

27. And as concerning thy not returning into the body thy days are not yet fulfilled for coming here."

28. And when I heard (that) I was troubled, and he said: "Do not be troubled."

CHAPTER 9

AND he took me into the air of the seventh heaven, and moreover I heard a voice saying: "How far will he ascend that dwelleth in the flesh?" And I feared and trembled.

2. And when I trembled, behold, I heard from hence another voice being sent forth, and saying: "It is permitted to the holy Isaiah to ascend hither; for here is his garment."

3. And I asked the angel who was with me and said: "Who is he who forbade me and who is he who permitted me to ascend?"

4. And he said unto me: "He who forbade thee, is he who is over the praise-giving of the sixth heaven.

5. And He who permitted thee, this is thy Lord God, the Lord Christ, who will be called "Jesus" in the world, but His name thou canst not hear till thou hast ascended out of thy body."

6. And he raised me up into the seventh heaven, and I saw there a wonderful light and angels innumerable.

7. And there I saw the holy Abel and all the righteous.

8. And there I saw Enoch and all who were with him, stript of the garments of the flesh, and I saw them in their garments of the upper world, and they were like angels, standing there in great glory.

9. And there I saw Enoch and all who were with him, stript of the garments of the flesh, and I saw them in their garments of the upper world, and they were like angels, standing there in great glory.

10. But they sat not on their thrones, nor were their crowns of glory on them.

11. And I asked the angel who was with me: "How is it that they have received the garments, but have not the thrones and the crowns?"

12. And he said unto me: "Crowns and thrones of glory they do not receive, till the Beloved will descent in the form in which you will see Him descent [will descent, I say] into the world in the last days the Lord, who will be called Christ.

13. Nevertheless they see and know whose will be thrones, and whose the crowns when He has descended and been made in your form, and they will think that He is flesh and is a man.

14. And the god of that world will stretch forth his hand against the Son, and they will crucify Him on a tree, and will slay Him not knowing who He is.

15. And thus His descent, as you will see, will be hidden even from the heavens, so that it will not be known who He is.

16. And when He hath plundered the angel of death, He will ascend on the third day, [and he will remain in that world five hundred and forty-five days].

17. And then many of the righteous will ascend with Him, whose spirits do not receive their garments till the Lord Christ ascend and they ascend with Him.

18. Then indeed they will receive their [garments and] thrones and crowns, when He has ascended into the seventh heaven."

19. And I said unto him that which I had asked him in the third heaven:

20. "Show me how everything which is done in that world is here made known."

21. And whilst I was still speaking with him, behold one of the angels who stood nigh, more glorious than the glory of that angel, who had raised me up from the world.

22. Showed me a book, [but not as a book of this world] and he opened it, and the book was written, but not as a book of this world. And he gave (it) to me and I read it, and lo! the deeds of the children of Israel were written therein, and the deeds of those whom I know (not), my son Josab.

23. And I said: "In truth, there is nothing hidden in the seventh heaven, which is done in this world."

24. And I saw there many garments laid up, and many thrones and many crowns.

25. And I said to the angel: "Whose are these garments and thrones and crowns?"

26. And he said unto me: "These garments many from that world will receive, believing in the words of That One, who shall be named as I told thee, and they will observe those things, and believe in them, and believe in His cross: for them are these laid up."

27. And I saw a certain One standing, whose glory surpassed that of all, and His glory was great and wonderful.

28. And after I had seen Him, all the righteous whom I had seen and also the angels whom I had seen came to Him. And Adam and Abel and Seth and all the righteous first drew near and worshipped Him, and they all praised Him with one voice, and I myself also gave praise with them, and my giving of praise was as theirs.

29. And then all the angels drew nigh and worshipped and gave praise.

30. And I was (again) transformed and became like an angel.

31. And thereupon the angel who conducted me said to me: "Worship this One," and I worshipped and praised.

32. And the angel said unto me: "This is the Lord of all the praise-givings which thou hast seen."

33. And whilst he was still speaking, I saw another Glorious One who was like Him, and the righteous drew nigh and worshipped and praised, and I praised together with them. But my glory was not transformed into accordance with their form.

34. And thereupon the angels drew near and worshipped Him.

35. And I saw the Lord and the second angel, and they were standing.

36. And the second whom I saw was on he left of my Lord. And I asked: "Who is this?" and he said unto me: "Worship Him, for He is the angel of the Holy Spirit, who speaketh in thee and the rest of the righteous."

37. And I saw the great glory, the eyes of my spirit being open, and I could not thereupon see, nor yet could the angel who was with me, nor all the angels whom I had seen worshipping my Lord.

38. But I saw the righteous beholding with great power the glory of that One.

39. And my Lord drew nigh to me and the angel of the Spirit and He said: "See how it is given to thee to see God, and on thy account power is given to the angel who is with thee."

40. And I saw how my Lord and the angel of the Spirit worshipped, and they both together praised God.

41. And thereupon all the righteous drew near and worshipped.

42. And the angels drew near and worshipped and all the angels praised.

CHAPTER 10

AND thereupon I heard the voices and the giving of praise, which I had heard in each of the six heavens, ascending and being heard there:

2. And all were being sent up to that Glorious One whose glory I could not behold.

3. And I myself was hearing and beholding the praise (which was given) to Him.

4. And the Lord and the angel of the Spirit were beholding all and hearing all.

5. And all the praises which are sent up from the six heavens are not only heard, but seen.

6. And I heard the angel who conducted me and he said: "This is the Most High of the high ones, dwelling in the holy world, and resting in His holy ones, who will be called by the Holy Spirit through the lips of the righteous the Father of the Lord."

7. And I heard the voice of the Most High, the Father of my Lord, saying to my Lord Christ who will be called Jesus:

8. "Go forth and descent through all the heavens, and thou wilt descent to the firmament and that world: to the angel in Sheol thou wilt descend, but to Haguel thou wilt not go.

9. And thou wilt become like unto the likeness of all who are in the five heavens.

10. And thou wilt be careful to become like the form of the angels of the firmament [and the angels also who are in Sheol].

11. And none of the angels of that world shall know that Thou art with Me of the seven heavens and of their angels.

12. And they shall not know that Thou art with Me, till with a loud voice I have called (to) the heavens, and their angels and their lights, (even) unto the sixth heaven, in order that you mayest judge and destroy the princes and angels and gods of that world, and the world that is dominated by them:

13. For they have denied Me and said: "We alone are and there is none beside us."

14. And afterwards from the angels of death Thou wilt ascend to Thy place. And Thou wilt not be transformed in each heaven, but in glory wilt Thou ascend and sit on My right hand.

15. And thereupon the princes and powers of that world will worship Thee."

16. These commands I heard the Great Glory giving to my Lord.

17. And so I saw my Lord go forth from the seventh heaven into the sixth heaven.

18. And the angel who conducted me [from this world was with me and] said unto me: "Understand, Isaiah, and see the transformation and descent of the Lord will appear."

19. And I saw, and when the angels saw Him, thereupon those in the sixth heaven praised and lauded Him; for He had not been transformed after the shape of the angels there, and they praised Him and I also praised with them.

20. And I saw when He descended into the fifth heaven, that in the fifth heaven He made Himself like unto the form of the angels

there, and they did not praise Him (nor worship Him); for His form was like unto theirs.

21. And then He descended into the forth heaven, and made Himself like unto the form of the angels there.

22. And when they saw Him, they did not praise or laud Him; for His form was like unto their form.

23. And again I saw when He descended into the third heaven, and He made Himself like unto the form of the angels in the third heaven.

24. And those who kept the gate of the (third) heaven demanded the password, and the Lord gave (it) to them in order that He should not be recognized. And when they saw Him, they did not praise or laud Him; for His form was like unto their form.

25. And again I saw when He descended into the second heaven, and again He gave the password there; those who kept the gate proceeded to demand and the Lord to give.

26. And I saw when He made Himself like unto the form of the angels in the second heaven, and they saw Him and they did not praise Him; for His form was like unto their form.

27. And again I saw when He descended into the first heaven, and there also He gave the password to those who kept the gate, and He made Himself like unto the form of the angels who were on the left of that throne, and they neither praised nor lauded Him; for His form was like unto their form.

28. But as for me no one asked me on account of the angel who conducted me.

29. And again He descended into the firmament where dwelleth the ruler of this world, and He gave the password to those on the left, and His form was like theirs, and they did not praise Him there; but they were envying one another and fighting; for here there is a power of evil and envying about trifles.

30. And I saw when He descended and made Himself like unto the angels of the air, and He was like one of them.

31. And He gave no password; for one was plundering and doing violence to another.

CHAPTER 11

AFTER this I saw, and the angel who spoke with me, who conducted me, said unto me: "Understand, Isaiah son of Amoz; for for this purpose have I been sent from God."

2. And I indeed saw a woman of the family of David the prophet, named Mary, and Virgin, and she was espoused to a man named Joseph, a carpenter, and he also was of the seed and family of the righteous David of Bethlehem Judah.

3. And he came into his lot. And when she was espoused, she was found with child, and Joseph the carpenter was desirous to put her away.

4. But the angel of the Spirit appeared in this world, and after that Joseph did not put her away, but kept Mary and did not reveal this matter to any one.

5. And he did not approach May, but kept her as a holy virgin, though with child.

6. And he did not live with her for two months.

7. And after two months of days while Joseph was in his house, and Mary his wife, but both alone.

8. It came to pass that when they were alone that Mary straightway looked with her eyes and saw a small babe, and she was astonished.

9. And after she had been astonished, her womb was found as formerly before she had conceived.

10. And when her husband Joseph said unto her: "What has astonished thee?" his eyes were opened and he saw the infant and praised God, because into his portion God had come.

11. And a voice came to them: "Tell this vision to no one."

12. And the story regarding the infant was noised broad in Bethlehem.

13. Some said: "The Virgin Mary hath borne a child, before she was married two months."

14. And many said: "She has not borne a child, nor has a midwife gone up (to her), nor have we heard the cries of (labour) pains." And they were all blinded respecting Him and they all knew regarding Him, though they knew not whence He was.

15. And they took Him, and went to Nazareth in Galilee.

16. And I saw, O Hezekiah and Josab my son, and I declare to the other prophets also who are standing by, that (this) hath escaped all the heavens and all the princes and all the gods of this world.

17. And I saw: In Nazareth He sucked the breast as a babe and as is customary in order that He might not be recognized.

18. And when He had grown up he worked great signs and wonders in the land of Israel and of Jerusalem.

19. And after this the adversary envied Him and roused the children of Israel against Him, not knowing who He was, and they delivered Him to the king, and crucified Him, and He descended to the angel (of Sheol).

20. In Jerusalem indeed I was Him being crucified on a tree:

21. And likewise after the third day rise again and remain days.

22. And the angel who conducted me said: "Understand, Isaiah": and I saw when He sent out the Twelve Apostles and ascended.

23. And I saw Him, and He was in the firmament, but He had not changed Himself into their form, and all the angels of the firmament and the Satans saw Him and they worshipped.

24. And there was much sorrow there, while they said: "How did our Lord descend in our midst, and we perceived not the glory [which has been upon Him], which we see has been upon Him from the sixth heaven?"

25. And He ascended into the second heaven, and He did not transform Himself, but all the angels who were on the right and on the left and the throne in the midst.

26. Both worshipped Him and praised Him and said: "How did our Lord escape us whilst descending, and we perceived not?"

27. And in like manner He ascended into the third heaven, and they praised and said in like manner.

28. And in the fourth heaven and in the fifth also they said precisely after the same manner.

29. But there was one glory, and from it He did not change Himself.

30. And I saw when He ascended into the sixth heaven, and they worshipped and glorified Him.

31. But in all the heavens the praise increased (in volume).

32. And I saw how He ascended into the seventh heaven, and all the righteous and all the angels praised Him. And then I saw Him

sit down on the right hand of that Great Glory whose glory I told you that I could not behold.

33. And also the angel of the Holy Spirit I saw sitting on the left hand.

34. And this angel said unto me: "Isaiah, son of Amoz, it is enough for thee;... for thou hast seen what no child of flesh has seen.

35. And thou wilt return into thy garment (of the flesh) until thy days are completed. Then thou wilt come hither."

36. These things Isaiah saw and told unto all that stood before him, and they praised. And he spake to Hezekiah the King and said: "I have spoken these things."

37. Both the end of this world;

38. And all this vision will be consummated in the last generations.

39. And Isaiah made him swear that he would not tell (it) to the people of Israel, nor give these words to any man to transcribe.

40. ...such things ye will read. and watch ye in the Holy Spirit in order they ye may receive your garments and thrones and crowns of glory which are laid up in the seventh heaven.

41. On account of these visions and prophecies Sammael Satan sawed in sunder Isaiah the son of Amoz, the prophet, by the hand of Manasseh.

42. And all these things Hezekiah delivered to Manasseh in the twenty-sixth year.

43. But Manasseh did not remember them nor place these things in his heart, but becoming the servant of Satan he was

destroyed. Here endeth the vision of Isaiah the prophet with his ascension.

www.ingramcontent.com/pod-product-compliance
Lightning Source LLC
LaVergne TN
LVHW041501070426
835507LV00009B/743